Little Computer Scientists

Teach your child or student basic computer science concepts and vocabulary and leave them clamoring for more!

Beautifully illustrated and engagingly written, *Little Computer Scientists* is a whimsical exploration of computer science concepts for kids! Join a group of amateur coders as they work in binary, debug code, use HTML to build a website, and even create a LAN to game together. Using a captivating story and a diverse cast of characters, this picture book will introduce children to pertinent vocabulary and essential concepts needed to inspire an interest in computer science.

Consider the companion guidebook *Supporting the Development of Computer Science Concepts in Early Childhood* to help dig even deeper, engender excitement, and provide a solid understanding of computer science that sets your learner up for future success!

For effective use, this book should be purchased alongside the guidebook. The guidebook, *Little Computer Scientists*, and an additional storybook, *Little Hackers*, can be purchased together as a set, *Developing Computer Science Concepts in Early Childhood* [978-1-032-47108-2].

Julie Darling is a teacher/librarian at the Ann Arbor STEAM school. She has a Master of Science in Information from the University of Michigan and is a Raspberry Pi certified educator. Julie has been teaching technology for more than 20 years.

D. J. Cools is a writer, illustrator, and designer with a passion for books, outdoor adventure, and old cars. Originally from Washington State, D. J. enjoys cycling, exploring, and small-town family life in Southeastern Michigan.

Little Computer Scientists

Written by
Julie Darling

Illustrated by
D. J. Cools

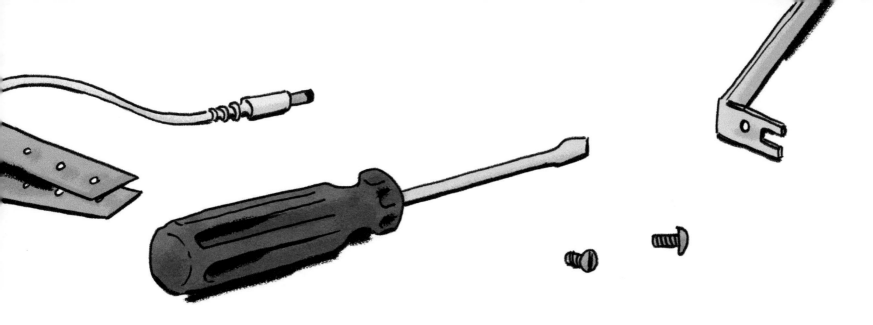

First published 2025
by Routledge
605 Third Avenue, New York, NY 10158

and by Routledge
4 Park Square, Milton Park, Abingdon, Oxon, OX14 4RN

Routledge is an imprint of the Taylor & Francis Group, an informa business

Library of Congress Cataloging-in-Publication Data
Names: Darling, Julie, author. | Cools, Darren, illustrator.
Title: Little computer scientists / Julie Darling; illustrated by Darren Cools.
Description: New York: Routledge, 2024.
Identifiers: LCCN 2024007017 (print) | LCCN 2024007018 (ebook) | ISBN 9781032471150 (pbk) | ISBN 9781003501510 (ebk)
Subjects: LCSH: Computer science—Juvenile literature. | Computer programming—Juvenile literature.

Classification: LCC QA76.23 .D38 2024 (print) | LCC QA76.23 (ebook) | DDC 004—dc23/eng/20240304
LC record available at https://lccn.loc.gov/2024007017
LC ebook record available at https://lccn.loc.gov/2024007018

ISBN: 978-1-032-47115-0 (pbk)
ISBN: 978-1-003-50151-0 (ebk)

DOI: 10.4324/9781003501510

Typeset in Calibri
by Deanta Global Publishing Services, Chennai, India

To my daughters, and my A2 STEAM students. My greatest hope is that you see yourselves reflected in these pages.

—Julie Darling

For Darrell and Dann, who introduced me to the magic of computers.

—D. J. Cools

My friends and I love computer science.

It's fun for everyone!

A	01000001	J	01001010	S	01010011
B	01000010	K	01001011	T	01010100
C	01000011	L	01001100	U	01010101
D	01000100	M	01001101	V	01010110
E	01000101	N	01001110	W	01010111
F	01000110	O	01001111	X	01011000
G	01000111	P	01010000	Y	01011001
H	01001000	Q	01010001	Z	01011010
I	01001001	R	01010010		

We love to use **binary** code.

01000001! (This is a capital A.)

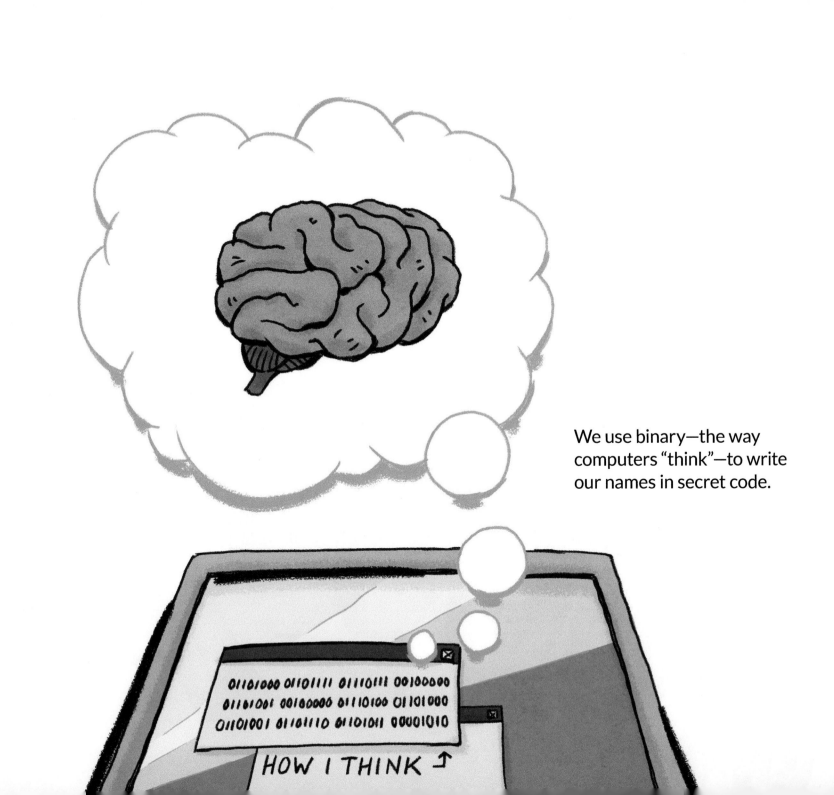

We use binary—the way computers "think"—to write our names in secret code.

Why don't you try it too?

We've only just begun!

Computers use lots of languages.

We'll start with just a few.

We use **Python** in the **command line** to tell the computer exactly what to do.

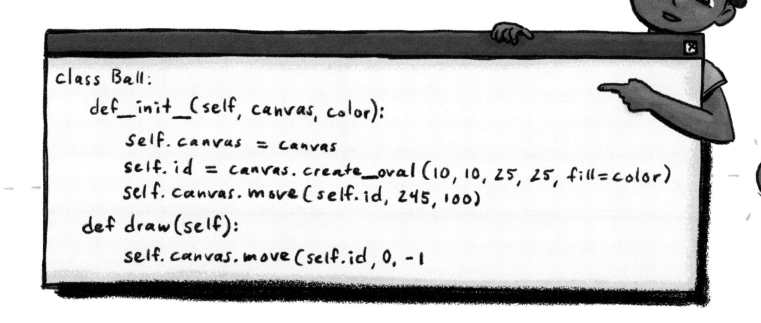

```
class Ball:
    def __init__(self, canvas, color):
        self.canvas = canvas
        self.id = canvas.create_oval(10, 10, 25, 25, fill=color)
        self.canvas.move(self.id, 245, 100)
    def draw(self):
        self.canvas.move(self.id, 0, -1
```

Debug the whole way through.

We try to run the program.

Oh no! An error message appears.

We worked so hard.

We'll persevere.

We must have missed a detail.

We re-read our code all through.

We missed that closing bracket.

```
class Ball:
    def __init__(self, canvas, color):
        self.canvas = canvas
        self.id = canvas.create_oval(10, 1 , 25, 25, fill=color)
        self.canvas.move(self.id, 245, 1  )
    def draw(self):
        self.canvas.move(self.id, 0, -1
```

Now we know just what to do!

We re-connect our
Raspberry Pis.

```
class Ball:
    def __init__(self, canvas, color):
        self.canvas = canvas
        self.id = canvas.create_oval(10, 10, 25, 25, fill=color)
        self.canvas.move(self.id, 245, 100)
    def draw(self):
        self.canvas.move(self.id, 0, -1)
```

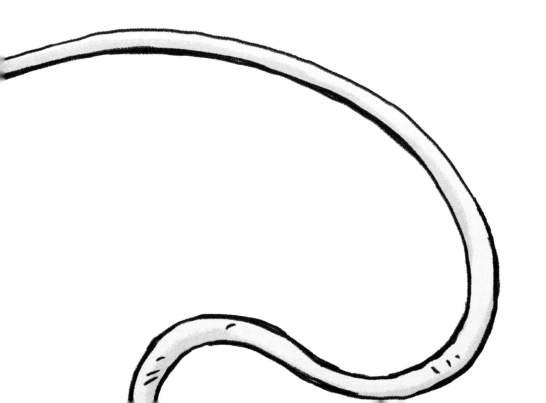

We run the code again.

The LEDs light up! It worked this time!

It's *so* much fun to code with friends.

We build a debugging website using **HTML** (HyperText Markup Language).

```
<header className={styles['header']}>
  <h1 className={styles['text-1']}>
    Troubleshoot Your Work
  </h1>
  <p className={styles['text-2']}>
    Copy and paste your code here to
    analyze it for errors.
  </p>
  <div className={styles['get-started1']}>
    <span className={styles['text-3']}>Get started</span>
  </div>
</header>
```

```
.container {
    width: 100%;
    display: flex;
    overflow: auto;
    min-height: 100vh;
    overflow-x: hidden;
    flex-direction: column;
}
```

We make our updates *cascade*
through by adding **CSS**
(Cascading Style Sheets), as well.

We set up a **Local Area Network** (*LAN*) so all our friends can play.

We build in Minecraft all together.

What a busy day!

Author's Note

Kids given exposure to pertinent vocabulary and essential concepts in any field of study are more likely to have success (and are more likely to be interested) in that discipline. This book (and its companion—*Little Hackers*) aims to do just that.

Here are more details about the vocabulary and concepts explored in this story.

Binary is the "language" of computers. It is made up of 1's (signal on) and 0's (signal off). Computer chips are made up of transistors that act like tiny switches. If an electrical current is flowing through the transistor, it is a signal on, or 1. If no electrical current is flowing through the transistor, it is a signal off, or 0. Binary is also called "machine code". The central processing unit (CPU) of a computer can only understand information written in binary/machine code.

Python is a popular software coding language (named after the BBC comedy series *Monty Python's Flying Circus*). It has many applications including: artificial intelligence, machine learning, game design, creating websites and data analytics, making it quite versatile. Python is considered a "high-level" programming language, which means it's easy for people to read and write. This is part of what makes it a good programming language for beginners. In addition, you can run each line of code to check for errors, making it easier to debug. A good progression for kids learning to code is to start with ScratchJr, progress to Scratch, and then explore Python and/or HTML/CSS.

The command line is a way to type instructions directly into the computer (instead of using your mouse to click and select from a drop-down menu). This text-interface often allows you to work more quickly and gives you more control over your computer.

Debugging is finding and fixing mistakes or problems in computer programs.

Raspberry Pi is an inexpensive personal computer that can fit in the palm of your hand. There are a variety of accessories that you can connect to your Raspberry Pi. Some of these are for usability: for example, a power supply, monitor, mouse, keyboard, and micro-SD card. Some of these are for innovation: for example, a camera or the "Sense Hat" which allows you to track your environment for variations in pressure, humidity, movement, and more, and use the built-in LEDs (light-emitting diodes, which look like little light bulbs, but are actually considered tiny semiconductors) to see this data. Python is a good language to use with a Raspberry Pi (you can also use Scratch).

HTML (HyperText Markup Language) and **CSS** (Cascading Style Sheets) are the basic building blocks of web design. HTML is used to structure the content of web pages; CSS is used to format the content that will then cascade through the whole page (as opposed to having to make changes on each line of code). For example, if all the title headings on your page are green and you want to change them to purple, you can use CSS to do that—quickly!

LAN stands for **Local Area Network**. This is a way of connecting devices together to form a network. It's often used to allow several people to access the same information. One intriguing use of a LAN is to set one up so that your kids can play Minecraft with their friends. As they get older, they can learn to do this themselves. Another example of a LAN is a Wi-Fi router in a house. This is a LAN that connects the devices that you use at home which could include computers, televisions, smart speakers, smart thermostats, smart appliances, etc.

If you'd like more resources for teaching your littles the basics of computer science, consider pairing *Little Computer Scientists* with *Little Hackers* and *Supporting the Development of Computer Science Concepts in Early Childhood: A Practical Guide for Parents and Educators*. Together, these books will help you to give your little ones a solid foundational knowledge base for understanding and excelling at computer science.